Thanks for purchasing this book! I [...] it. For even more Web search tips, tricks, and digital how-to's, visit www.websearchsecrets.com. I've been helping hundreds of thousands of people all over the world learn how to use the Internet more efficiently since 2004 – I invite you to join us!

Thanks again!

- *Web Search Secrets Wendy*

101 Ways to Find Free Books Online

Get Reading Suggestions for Your Next Book

Find out what book would be best for your tastes with <u>What Should I Read Next</u>, a great way to get reading suggestions. Simply enter in a book or author that you really like and What Should I Read Next will use its sizable database (20,000 books at the time of this writing) to figure out what authors

and/or books are most likely going to be compatible with your reading preferences.
For instance, I input "Divine Secrets of the Ya-Ya Sisterhood", one of my favorite books, and got some great recommendations for the next time I visit the library.

Thain's Book

a Middle Earth encyclopedia

For all you Lord of the Rings fans: "Welcome to The Thain's Book, an encyclopedia of the people, places, creatures, things, and events in The Hobbit and The Lord of the Rings by J.R.R. Tolkien. Entries include descriptions, histories, important dates, genealogies, etymologies, illustrations, sources and cross-references."

Five Sources for Free Textbooks

If you haven't checked the prices of college textbooks lately, you're probably in for quite a shock. For most students, one of the most expensive items on their university to-do list is simply purchasing the books they will need for their chosen classes. Not only are these books exorbitantly priced, they also command a very low exchange rate when returned at the end of the semester. What's a poor college student to do?

Well, there are free online textbook sources, however, not every textbook in every single college class is necessarily offered there. Enter textbook rentals, a cheap Web alternative to the high price of college textbooks.

How does renting a textbook online work?

For the most part, Web textbook rentals work like this: you type in the name of your book or the ISBN number (the ISBN number is going to return you more accurate results since it's a unique identification number; this is preferred especially for different editions of textbooks that might have very similar names but different content), you pay a small fee (much less than the cost of purchasing the book), and then the book is either delivered to you via mail or you can read the book in your Web browser, a method that is quite convenient since you can usually transfer it to other devices such as your smartphone, tablet, or other mobile device.

If you search for "textbook rentals" on the Web, you'll come up with quite a few results. However, here are the top five that deliver the most consistent experiences according to user reviews and customer confidence.

Amazon

It's only logical that Amazon offers textbook rentals, simply because they are the world's largest and most popular online book retailer. Visit Amazon Textbook Rentals and you're presented with a wide variety of textbook categories, anything from Accounting to Visual Arts. The process is simple: find the books you need, take advantage of free shipping if you're a student (some restrictions apply), keep your book for a semester, and then ship it back free when you're done.

College Book Renter

College Book Renter does one thing and one thing only: provide textbooks to students at a nominal fee. Here's how CBR works: find the book you need, choose how long you need it (you can keep it longer than just a semester if you need to), and then make your purchase. Your book will arrive in the mail soon after.

If you decide you'd rather purchase your book, you can do that too - and you can sell it back to CBR once you don't need it anymore.

Chegg

Chegg offers not only textbook rentals, but homework help, course planners, and buyback services. Renting a textbook here is easy: just type in the ISBN, figure out if you want a physical or ecopy of your book, and make your purchase. If for any reason you are not satisfied with your purchase, you have twenty-one days to return your book (fourteen days for an e-book).

Barnes and Noble

Barnes and Noble has one of the more comprehensive textbook selections in this list, with very flexible rental periods extending up to 130 days. Both new and used textbooks are available to rent, and free shipping is offered to customers once they decide they no longer need their items. Categories from Algebra to Test Prep are available here.

Your university

Many colleges and universities are starting to recognize that students need more textbook use options, and are therefore offering textbook rentals on campus. A simple search using Google can help you find out if your university offers this service:

"textbook rentals" site:www.myuniversity.edu

Substitute the name of your college or university for "myuniversity.edu", and you'll be able to find out if this is an option for you. Need a more generalized search? Try textbook rentals site:edu to see what colleges offer a cheaper textbook alternative.

Many Web-based options for students

As the Web evolves, we'll see more options like this for college students, making the prospect of higher education a less expensive one. Whether you're at university for the first time or you're returning after many years in the professional field and you're looking to make a change, it's nice to know that you have options when making these potentially very expensive purchases.

The Top Ten Websites for Bookworms

Whether you're looking for a textbook, a comic book, or a cookbook, the chances are very good that you'll find it with one of the book websites listed below. Buying books on the Web can end up in some serious savings, not to mention the amazing variety that is available to you.

The following sites offer books in a variety of formats:

- Instantly downloadable to your e-reader
- Full books available to read from within your Web browser
- Books that you can order and receive in the mail Whatever you're looking for, there's a good chance you'll be able to find it here.

Amazon

Amazon.com is one of the best places on the Web to begin your book search. You can find out of print books here, rare books, used textbooks, and much, much more. You can also use Amazon to find upcoming book titles or take advantage of coupons specifically for Amazon.

ReadPrint

ReadPrint is a free online library where you can find literally thousands of free books to read for free online, from classics to science fiction to Shakespeare. Download these books to your computer, your mobile device, or simply read them within your Web browser.

BookFinder.com

BookFinder holds over 100 million new, used, rare, and out of print books within its substantial index. This is a good place to find books from independent publishers, as well as books that had limited printings.

Google Book Search

Google Book Search allows you to search actual book text to find what interests you, and then gives you various places on the Web you can buy these books. Only text that is NOT copyrighted is searchable. Many free books are available here to read online as well as magazines, journals, and e-books.

Indie Store Finder

Simply enter in your zip code to Indie Store Finder, and you'll be taken to a list of more than 1200 independent bookstores across the USA who are plugged into this unique book search engine. It's an easy way to find a local book store near you that might carry interesting books you won't be able to find anywhere else.

Comic Book Resources

Comic Book Resources is a fantastic resource for comic book lovers; you can find information about both old and new comic books, as well as local comic book stores in your area. If you are a comic book aficionado, this is an excellent source for your favorite heroes and heroines.

AddAll.com

AddAll is a comparison shopping book search engine that you can use to search for books from an enormous selection compiled from many online booksellers. Search by title, shipping destination, state, and price.

Alibris

Alibris.com is a great place to find used books, used textbooks, rare books, out of print books, and more. If you're looking for books from independent publishers, this is one of the best resources online.

Online Book Search - University of Pennsylvania

The Online Books Page from the University of Pennsylvania allows the searcher to search and read actual online text of classic books. For example, a search for "Jane Austen" resulted in a huge list of everything Austen on the Web. Search results will give you links to where these works can be found in their entirety, as well as where they can be downloaded for free.

Powells

Powells Books has been around for about 33 years now, and you can find an extremely eclectic selection of books here, anything from historical novels to self-published books.

Rare Book Room

A collection of some of the world's most rare books

Read over four hundred of the world's most rare and wonderful books at the Rare Book Room, an online repository of such classics as the Shakespeare Quartos, the complete copies of Poor Richard's Almanac by Benjaman Franklin, and the first printing of the Bill of Rights.

Neiman Marcus Christmas Book

Some of the most expensive gifts you'll ever see

Find something you can't afford in the <u>Neiman Marcus Christmas Book</u>, a yearly offering that caters to those who can afford million dollar slippers (among other things).

CIA World Fact Book

An incredibly deep resource for world information

The <u>CIA World Fact Book</u> is a comprehensive resource for facts about every country in the world - geography, demographics, culture, and more.

Google Book Search

You can use <u>Google Book Search</u> to do a lot of things: find a book you're interested in, search within a book's text, download a book, search reference texts, even create your own Google Library of your favorite books.

Great Books Index

Large collection of classic books and supplementary resources

Looking for free online editions of classic books? Look no further than the Great Books Index, a large database of free online books, notes, and supplementary materials.

Bookslut

An online magazine just for book lovers

Bookslut is an insightful author interviews, commentary, and news from the world of book writing.

Friends of Ed Free Tech Books - Free Download

Grab a ton of free technology ebooks at Friends of Ed's free computer books downloads page.

BooksWellRead

A great place for book lovers

Get a free online journal about your favorite books at BooksWellRead: "designed for bookworms who want to share their reflections about what they read."

BookMooch

Swap books with other BookMooch members

Here's how BookMooch works: you volunteer the books that you'd like to give away, you then receive requests from other BookMooch members for those books, you mail your books and get points, and then you can redeem books from other people.

O'Reilly Open Books Project - Free Download

The O'Reilly Open Books Project is a great way to find some of the best tech books out there.

Free Web Books at the University of Adelaide

Download yourself a free book today

The University of Adelaide has made available a wonderful collection of free Web books, organzied by author, title, theme, and full-text.

Free Technical Books: Five Free Sources

There are plenty of sites out there that allow you download free, complete, computer books. Here are just a few of the sites you can find free computer books:

- Free Computer Books: Unix, Linux, even free computer magazines here available for download.
- FreeTechBooks:Computer books and lecture notes. This is a great place to go if you want to save on a textbook.
- Google Books: You can get limited previews of specific computer books here at Google Books.

- <u>Google Scholar</u>: If you know a specific author or you know exactly what you're looking for, try Google Scholar.

Free Books: How to Use Google to Uncover Great Reading Material

More people than ever before in history are using the Web as a free library, and with good reason: there are literally thousands of free books online that you can download in their entirety, listen to in an audio book version, or simply read within your browser window.

There are a couple different ways to accomplish this with Google.

First, let's try a simple search engine query. Because most books on the Web are formatted in .pdf form, we can search by file type. Let's try <u>Google</u>:

filetype:pdf "jane eyre"

This Google search brings back plenty of .pdf formatted files that reference the classic novel "Jane Eyre". However, not all of them are the actual book; quite a few of them are classroom notes or other such materials that just reference Jane Eyre.

We can use another kind of Google syntax to make our book search even more powerful - the allinurl command.

What is the "allinurl" command? It's similar to inurl with one crucial difference: allinurl will search ONLY the URL of a document or Web page, while inurl will look at both the URL and the content on the Web page. Note: the "allinurl" command can not be combined with other Google search commands (such as "filetype"), but there's a way around this.

Using the allinurl command, basic search math,quotations, and parentheses for control over exactly which file formats you're looking for, you can tell Google to return the complete work of

"Jane Eyre", rather than just excerpts or discussions.

Let's see how this would work:

allinurl: +(|zip|pdf|doc) "jane eyre"

Here's how this particular search string breaks down:

The allinurl command tells Google that you only want to look at what's in the URL.

See that plus sign? That's basic search math, also known as Boolean search. You're telling Google that whatever comes after that plus sign needs to be included.

The parentheses and pipes look complicated, but they're really not. They're just grouping tools. The parentheses tell Google that you want to ONLY look at content that is delivered in these file formats, and the pipes separate those formats.

Since you are looking for more than one file type, they need to be separated by pipes (the pipe key is accessible on your keyboard right above the "Enter" key; just hit "shift" and that key and you'll get a pipe).

The title of your book inside quotation marks tells Google that you want to look for that entire title in exactly the way you've written it.

This Google search string will help you find all sorts of free books online. Feel free to experiment with it a little...add more file types, select other books, etc., and see what you can come up with!

Gutenberg Audio Books - Free Download
Download thousands of free classics

Download thousands of free classic audio books at the Gutenberg Audio Books Project. You can choose between human-read audio books, or books read by computers.

Authorama

Authorama offers up a good selection of free, high-quality books that you can read right in your browser or print out for later. These books are in the public domain, which means that they are freely accessible and allowed to be distributed; in other words, you don't need to worry if you're looking at something illegal here.

How do I find books to read here?

Authorama is a very simple site to use.

You can scroll down the list of alphabetically arranged authors on the front page, or check out the list of Latest Additions at the top.

Once you find something you're interested in, click on the book title and you'll be taken to that book's specific page. You can choose to read chapters within your browser (easiest) or print pages out for later.

Why should I use this site?

If you're looking for an easy to use source of free books online, Authorama definitely fits the bill. All of the books offered here are classic, well-written literature, simple to find and simple to read.

ManyBooks

ManyBooks is one of the best resources for free books in a variety of download formats that you can possibly find on the Web. There are hundreds of books available here, in all sorts of interesting genres, and all of them are completely free.

How can I find books here?

ManyBooks makes it easy to find what you're looking for. You can search for books by:

- author
- title
- subject
- language
- most popular
- reader reviews
- recommendations

Plus, ManyBooks has put together collections of books that are an interesting way to explore topics in a more organized way, or you can check out the ManyBooks series page to get stories chronologically.

More advanced search options:

In addition to the options I've already laid out for you, you can also use ManyBooks Advanced Search to pinpoint exactly what you're looking for.

There's also the ManyBooks RSS feeds that can keep you up to date on a variety of new content, including: All New Titles.

How can I download books?

First, you'll need to choose which format you want to download your book in. Each book's page comes with a dropdown menu of dozens of different file formats, anything from a zip file to a .PDF file to a format suitable for most any mobile device out on the market today. Once you've figured out your format, just click on the download button and you're off and running.

Why ManyBooks is a good place to get free books

With over 20,000 books available, ManyBooks is an excellent place to find free books, especially if you've been looking for a good site to build up your mobile book selection.

I highly recommend ManyBooks as a quality, reputable website.

ReadPrint

What is ReadPrint?

ReadPrint is a free online library where you can find literally thousands of free books to read for free online, from classics to science fiction to Shakespeare.

All ReadPrint books are full-length, and divided by chapter. You can read these books right inside your browser. If you are searching for a specific section of a book, each book page offers you the option of searching within the book's content.

If you find a book you really like and you'd like to download it to your mobile e-reader, you can do that too; ReadPrint provides links to every book they offer at Amazon, where the book can be instantly downloaded.

How to find books

Searching for books at ReadPrint is wonderfully simple. There are three ways you can find what you're looking for at ReadPrint:

- By title (try entering it in the ReadPrint search box)
- By author (they are all alphabetically ordered)
- By checking out the Most Recently Added books on the ReadPrint front page.
  The books are also divided by author, so if you'd like to go straight to the Shakespeare section, you can: all the Shakespeare works are divided by genre in one convenient place.

Why should I use ReadPrint to find books?

ReadPrint is one of the best resources you possibly use online to find free online books. There are new books added on a regular basis, and books and author information are extremely easy to find and read.

In addition, it's extremely convenient to be able to instantly call up a classic novel or other free, public domain literature within your Web browser. ReadPrint makes finding free books easy and fun.

ReadPrint - A Great Site for Bibliophiles

ReadPrint is a site that gives readers all over the world a chance to populate their personal libraries with hundreds of thousands of free books in genres from Science Fiction to Romance.

Registration (it's free) at ReadPrint gives the user a virtual library card for a wide variety of books, as well as the ability to keep track of what you've read and what you'd like to read, discover new books you might like, and join online book clubs to discuss great works of literature.

There are several ways you can find what you're looking for at ReadPrint:

- A keyword search for book titles, authors, or quotes
- Search by type of work published; i.e., essays, fiction, non-fiction, plays, etc.
- View the top books to read online as per the ReadPrint community
- Browse the alphabetical author index
- Check out the top 250 most famous authors on ReadPrint

Once you've found a book you're interested in, you can click "Read Online" and the book will open within your Web browser. You can also write a review of the book, add it to your ReadPrint favorites, or recommend it to a friend.

In addition to an impressive array of free works of literature, ReadPrint also offers a comprehensive quotation database culled from authors on the site. You can search for quotes by individual author here, or, you can search by subject (Love, Friendship, Success, etc.).

20 Sources for Free Books Online

Ever thought of creating a library with thousands of books, and never spending a dime? Sounds impossible, but it's not! Freely available books in nearly any subject you can think of abound on the Web, ready to be read, downloaded, and shared. Here are the top twenty sites where you can find a wide variety of completely free books, anything from romance novels to computer technology manuals.

ReadPrint.com offers thousands of free books, including novels, poems, fiction, nonfiction, essays, and plays. They were voted one of Time magazine's best 50 websites in 2010, and for good reason: the site is easy to navigate, and there are over 8000 books here to download for free. The front page offers several different ways to find books, but my personal favorite is browsing through the list of Top Authors; notable picks include Louisa May Alcott, Rudyard Kipling, and Jack London.

ManyBooks: Check out the most popular titles, special collections, or browse through some covers to see what interests you. ManyBooks offers over 29,000 **free ebooks in a wide range** of categories, from Adventure to Young Readers. Browse through the most popular downloads, recommendations, and special collections.

The Literature Network: This site is organized alphabetically by author. Click on any author's name, and you'll see a biography, related links and articles, quizzes, and forums. Most of the literature here is free; some downloads require a small fee.

Free Computer Books: Every computer subject and programming language you can think of is represented here. Free books and **textbooks**, as well as extensive lecture notes, are available.

Librivox.org: Librivox is a dream come true for audiobook lovers. All the books here are absolutely free, which is good news for those of us who have had to pony up ridiculously high fees for substandard audiobooks. Librivox has many volunteers that work to release quality recordings of classic books, all free for anyone to download. If you've been looking for a great place to find free audio books, Librivox is a good place to start.

Authorama.com: Authorama features a nice selection of books written in HTML and XHTML, which basically means that they are in easily readable format. Most books here are featured in English, but there are quite a few German language texts as well. Books are organized alphabetically by the author's last name. Authorama offers a good selection of free books from a variety of authors, both current and classic.

Project Gutenberg: Project Gutenberg is one of the largest sources for free books on the Web, with over 30,000 free downloadable ebooks available in a wide variety of formats. Project Gutenberg is the oldest (and quite possibly the largest) library on the Web, with literally hundreds of thousands books available for free download. The vast majority of books at Project Gutenberg are released in English, but there are other languages available.
If you already know what you are looking for, search the database by author name, title,

language, or subjects. You can also check out the top 100 list to see what other people have been downloading.

Scribd offers a fascination collection of all kinds of reading materials: presentations, textbooks, popular reading, and much more, all organized by topic. Scribd is one of the Web's largest sources of published content, with literally millions of documents published every month.

International Digital Children's Library: Browse through a wide selection of high quality children's literature here. Check out Simple Search to get a big picture of how this library is organized: by age, reading level, length of book, genres, and more.

Ebooks and Text Archives: From the Internet Archive; a library of fiction, popular books, children's books, historical texts and academic books.

World Public Library: Technically, the World Public Library is NOT free. But for a measly 8.95 a year, you can gain access to hundreds of thousands of books in over one hundred different languages.

They also have over one hundred different special collections ranging from American Lit to Western Philosophy. Worth a look. They also have what they call a Give Away Page, which is over two hundred of their most popular titles, audio books, technical books,a and books made into movies. Give the freebies a try, and if you really like their service, then you can choose to become a member and get the whole collection.

Questia Public Library: Questia has long been a favorite choice of librarians and scholars for research help. They also offer a world-class library of free books filled with classics, rarities, and textbooks. More than 5000 books are available for download here, alphabetized both by title and by author.

Wikisource: Online library of user-submitted and maintained content. At the time of this writing, over 200,000 pieces of content are available to read.

Wikibooks: Wikibooks is an open collection of (mostly) textbooks. Subjects range from Computing to Languages to Science; you can see all that Wikibooks has to offer in Books by Subject.

Be sure to check out the Featured Books section, which highlights books that the Wikibooks community at large believes to be "the best of what Wikibooks has to offer, and should inspire people to improve the quality of other books".

Bibliomania: Bibliomania gives readers over 2000 free classics, including literature book notes, author bios, book summaries, and study guides. Books are presented in chapter format.

The Open Library: There are over one million books here, all free, all available in PDF, ePub, Daisy, DjVu and ASCII text. You can search for ebooks specifically by checking the "show only ebooks" box under the main search box. Once you've found an ebook, you will see that it will be available in a variety of formats.

Sacred Texts: Sacred Texts contains the Web's largest collection of free books about religion, mythology, folklore and the esoteric in general.

Slideshare: Slideshare is an online forum where anyone can upload a digital presentation on any subject. Millions of people utilize SlideShare for research, sharing ideas, and learning about new technologies. SlideShare supports documents and PDF files, and all these are available for free download (after free registration).

Free eBooks: Free eBooks offers a wonderfully diverse variety of books, ranging from Advertising to Health to Web Design. Standard memberships (yes, you do have to register in order to download anything, but it only takes a minute) are free and allow members to access unlimited eBooks in HTML, but only five books every month in the PDF and TXT formats. A VIP membership here gives you unlimited access to any book you want, in any format.

The Online Books Page: Maintained by the University of Pennsylvania, this page lists over one MILLION free books free available for download in dozens of different formats.

Thanks for purchasing this book! I hope you enjoy it. For even more Web search tips, tricks, and digital how-to's, visit www.websearchsecrets.com. I've been helping hundreds of thousands of people all over the world learn how to use the Internet more efficiently since 2004 – I invite you to join us!

Thanks again!

- *Web Search Secrets Wendy*